BTEC
HEALTH AND SOCIAL CARE
ASSESSMENT GUIDE

Unit 4 SOCIAL INFLUENCES ON HEALTH AND WELLBEING

ELIZABETH RASHEED

HODDER
EDUCATION
AN HACHETTE UK COMPANY

The sample learner answers provided in this assessment guide are intended to give guidance on how a learner might approach generating evidence for each assessment criterion. Answers do not necessarily include all of the evidence required to meet each assessment criterion. Assessor comments intend to highlight how sample answers might be improved to help learners meet the requirements of the grading criterion but are provided as a guide only. Sample answers and assessor guidance have not been verified by Edexcel and any information provided in this guide should not replace your own internal verification process.

Any work submitted as evidence for assessment for this unit must be the learner's own. Submitting as evidence, in whole or in part, any material taken from this guide will be regarded as plagiarism. Hodder Education accepts no responsibility for learners plagiarising work from this guide that does or does not meet the assessment criteria.

The sample assignment briefs are provided as a guide to how you might assess the evidence required for all or part of the internal assessment of this Unit. They have not been verified or endorsed by Edexcel and should be internally verified through your own Lead Internal Verifier as with any other assignment briefs, and/or checked through the BTEC assignment checking service.

Orders: please contact Bookpoint Ltd, 130 Milton Park, Abingdon, Oxon OX14 4SB. Telephone: +44 (0)1235 827720. Fax: +44 (0)1235 400454. Lines are open from 9.00a.m. to 5.00p.m., Monday to Saturday, with a 24-hour message answering service. You can also order through our website www.hoddereducation.co.uk

If you have any comments to make about this, or any of our other titles, please send them to educationenquiries@hodder.co.uk

British Library Cataloguing in Publication Data

A catalogue record for this title is available from the British Library

ISBN: 978 1 444 1 89742

Published 2013

Impression number   10 9 8 7 6 5 4 3 2 1

Year   2016 2015 2014 2013

Copyright © 2013 Elizabeth Rasheed

Cover photo © compucow – iStockphoto.com

Typeset by Integra Software Services Pvt. Ltd., Pondicherry, India.

Printed in Dubai for Hodder Education,
an Hachette UK Company,
338 Euston Road,
London NW1 3BH

Contents

For attention of the learner

You are not allowed to copy any information from this book and use it as your own evidence. That would count as plagiarism, which is taken very seriously and may result in disqualification. If you are in any doubt at all please speak to your teacher.

Acknowledgments

Photo credits

The authors and publishers would like to thank the following for permission to reproduce material in this book:

p. 5 © Image Source / Alamy; p. 6 © Jacek Chabraszewski - Fotolia. com; p. 20 (top left) © Brand X/ Photolibrary Group Ltd; (bottom left) © WavebreakMediaMicro - Fotolia; (top right) © Andersen Ross / Digital Vision / Getty Images; (bottom right) © Monkey Business - Fotolia; p. 21 © Scott Griessel - Fotolia; p. 22 (right) © Lisa F. Young - Fotolia; p. 32 © ALAIN VERMEULEN - Fotolia; p. 33 © Alexander Raths - Fotolia; p. 34 © Eléonore H - Fotolia; p. 35 © Imagestate Media (John Foxx); p. 36 (left) © chagin - Fotolia; (right) © Yuri Arcurs - Fotolia; p. 37 © bertys30 - Fotolia.

Command words

You will find the following command words in the assessment criteria for each unit.

Analyse	Identify the factors that apply and state how these are related. Explain the importance of each one.
Assess	Give careful consideration to all the factors or events that apply and identify which are the most important or relevant.
Compare	Identify the main factors that apply in two or more situations and explain the similarities and differences or advantages and disadvantages.
Describe	Give a clear description that includes all the relevant features – think of it as 'painting a picture with words'.
Discuss	Consider different aspects of a topic and how they interrelate, and the extent to which they are important.
Evaluate	Bring together all the information and review it to form a conclusion. Give evidence for each of your views or statements.
Explain	Provide details and give reasons and/or evidence to support the arguments being made. Start by introducing the topic then give the 'how' or 'why'.
Summarise	Demonstrate an understanding of the key facts, and if possible illustrate with relevant examples.

UNIT 4
Social Influences on Health and Wellbeing

Unit 4: Social Influences on Health and Wellbeing is an internally assessed, optional, specialist unit with three learning aims:

- Learning aim A: Explore the effects of socialisation on the health and wellbeing of individuals.
- Learning aim B: Understand the influences that relationships have on the health and wellbeing of individuals.
- Learning aim C: Investigate the effects of social factors on the health and wellbeing of individuals.

The unit focuses on how social factors influence both our health and our wellbeing. In it we examine the development of beliefs about what is right and wrong and how relationships, social class, income and education affect health and wellbeing.

Learning aim A covers socialisation and how this can influence not only our health but also how we feel about ourselves. Learning aim B looks at the influence that relationships have on health and wellbeing. Finally, in learning aim C, we look at the effects of social factors such as social class, income and education on health and wellbeing.

Each learning aim is divided into two sections. The first section focuses on the content of the learning aim and each of the topics are covered. At the end of each section there are some knowledge recap questions to test your understanding of the subject. The answers for the knowledge recap questions can be found at the end of the guide.

The second section of each learning aim provides support with assessment by using evidence generated by a student, for each grading criterion, with feedback from an assessor. The assessor has highlighted where the evidence is sufficient to satisfy the grading criterion and provided developmental feedback when additional work is required.

At the end of the book are examples of assignment briefs for this unit. There is a sample assignment for each learning aim, and the tasks allow you to generate the evidence needed to meet all the assessment criteria in the unit.

Learning aim A

Explore the effects of socialisation on the health and wellbeing of individuals

Assessment criteria

2A.P1 Explain the influence of agents of primary and secondary socialisation.

2A.P2 Describe the effects of socialisation on the health and wellbeing of individuals.

2A.M1 Explain the effects of primary and secondary socialisation on the health and wellbeing of individuals, with reference to relevant examples.

2A.D1 Evaluate the impact of primary and secondary socialisation on the health and wellbeing of individuals, with reference to relevant examples.

Primary and secondary socialisation

There are two types of socialisation:

- Primary socialisation, which is the first way babies learn how to interact with people
- Secondary socialisation, which is the way that a young person learns about the world from others outside the immediate family.

Socialisation does not happen if a baby is totally isolated. Socialisation only happens when others (agents) show the individual how to behave. This can be directly, by parents saying 'thank you' to teach a baby to be polite, or it can be indirectly, through media influence, for example when a child watches a violent cartoon then hits his baby brother.

Primary socialisation

Studied

The agents of primary socialisation are parents, brothers and sisters, and grandparents – whoever cares for the baby. They influence how the baby learns to speak, how the baby develops beliefs about the world, and the values of what is acceptable and not acceptable.

Figure 1.1 Primary socialisation

Secondary socialisation

The agents of secondary socialisation are:

- **friends and peers** – they may shape a person's behaviour
- **the media** – for example, advertising, social networking, television, celebrity culture, music, newspapers and magazines. These may influence what music a person listens to, or who they admire
- **other agents outside the immediate circle** – including early years workers at nursery or playgroup, then later on, teachers, youth workers, representatives of religions, work colleagues, social workers. These influence how a young person develops ideas of how to interact with others.

Figure 1.2 Secondary socialisation

Effects of socialisation

Gender roles

Gender roles are shaped by the expectations of male and female behaviour that our family and our friends have. In some cultures, boys are expected to play football but girls are expected to play with dolls. The girls who want to play football and the boys who want to play with dolls are made to feel abnormal. This negatively affects their wellbeing. Some people are challenging this traditional view and raising their children to join in with everything with a positive sense of wellbeing.

Attitudes

Socialisation shapes the way we think about things. If parents are willing to see people as individuals rather than 'the immigrant next door', their tolerance will shape their child's thinking. If on the other hand parents are prejudiced, the child will also learn to be prejudiced. Attitudes to religion and authority are transmitted through socialisation. If families respect religious leaders and authority figures such as teachers and police, then their children will learn to do the same. Later, secondary socialisation may change attitudes; a young person brought up to respect others may be influenced by friends who think it is fun to mock older people and the young person may adopt that behaviour.

Development of social norms and use of language

Socialisation affects the development of social norms and values, views of right and wrong, manners and behaviour. Norms are what people consider normal in that society. What choices people make about how to behave are influenced by their socialisation. Primary socialisation may have taught some to grab what they can, regardless of who owns it. This is the norm for them. Some people will join in a riot because they feel it is acceptable to break windows and loot shops. They may swear at the police. Others will move away and not join in. These choices are the result of socialisation. At times secondary socialisation changes what we learn through primary socialisation, so a rioter can change and become a model citizen.

The use of language is affected first of all by primary socialisation. We learn to speak the language our parents and family speak, whether it is English, Urdu or Spanish. We copy their accent and dialect, so someone from the north of England may speak English differently to a person from the south. Whether we swear or not as a child is influenced by our primary socialisation. Later, secondary socialisation may also influence our language. We learn new words as we become more educated, and develop specialist language as a result of secondary socialisation. Garage, grunge and rap are specialist words for music that may need to be explained to parents. We use words with friends that we do not use at home, and we use words in school essays that we do not use with friends. Secondary socialisation gives us a variety of languages to communicate with a variety of people.

Figure 1.3 How would you describe this band?

Influence on lifestyle choices

Socialisation influences lifestyle choices. Primary socialisation affects whether we are involved in sport. If mum and dad take their children swimming every weekend, the children are more likely to be able to swim and may get involved in other sports, but if mum and dad are working and the children are left to watch television, they are less likely to be involved in sport or take regular exercise.

Figure 1.4 Children are more likely to take part in sport if their parents are also involved

Whether we get a job or remain unemployed, and what careers we choose, are influenced by family and wider society. A child born into a family where no one has worked for three generations is less likely to become a doctor than one born into a family where grandparents, mother and father are all doctors. This is because of the influence of socialisation on lifestyle choices. To become a doctor needs hard work and determination, values which are instilled in early childhood. A young person also needs to have access to books and to be encouraged and supported to achieve. This attitude may not be there in a family that has opted to live totally on benefits for several generations.

The use and choice of medical care and treatment is also influenced by socialisation. Jehovah's Witnesses believe that we should not take blood and so refuse blood transfusions. This can at times pose a risk to life. Some people believe they have a right to decide when to end their own life, especially if they have a painful incurable disease. In this country it is illegal to do so and it is illegal to help someone to do so. Some of these people go abroad to make sure they can end their life when they wish.

Whether we take illegal drugs, stay faithful to a long-term partner, smoke, drink too much alcohol or attend a place of worship are all influenced by socialisation. It affects the choices we make about how to live. Some people adopt alternative lifestyles, perhaps living in a commune with a group of like-minded people, or they may try to live a more spiritual life by joining a religious community. Some people try to respect the planet and not waste resources or cause unnecessary pollution, so they may use public transport, recycle what they can and grow their own food. All these lifestyle choices are influenced by socialisation and some of these alternative practices are now becoming the norm.

Knowledge recap questions

1. What is socialisation?
2. What is primary socialisation?
3. What is secondary socialisation?
4. What aspects of life does socialisation affect?

Assessment guidance for learning aim A

Scenario

You are helping at a local youth club and the organisers want young people to be aware of the effect of socialisation on health and wellbeing. They have asked you to write short stories based on fictional characters to show this. Your work will need to explore the effects of socialisation on the health and wellbeing of individuals.

2A.P1 **Explain the influence of agents of primary and secondary socialisation.**

Assessor report: The command verb in the grading criteria is **explain**. In the learner's answers we would expect to see details and reasons and/or evidence to support the arguments being made. The learner should start by introducing the topic, then give the 'how' or 'why'.

✎ Learner answer

Socialisation is the process of learning to interact with others in society. Babies who are isolated from others at birth, if they survived, would not be socialised. Agents of socialisation are the means by which we are socialised. Usually agents of socialisation are people, but the media, television and other forms of communication such as social media have a role to play in secondary socialisation **(a)**.

Agents of primary socialisation are those people who care for us, our parents or carers, sometimes our grandparents or brothers and sisters. They show us how to interact. A mother smiles at her baby and the baby learns to smile back. The father baths the baby and shows him how to splash and enjoy water, so the baby develops confidence and is not scared of water. This is how agents of primary socialisation influence us **(b)**. They do this so that the child will grow and be accepted as part of that society **(d)**.

Agents of secondary socialisation are those influences — usually people — outside the immediate family, for example, teachers and friends. Television is increasingly an agent of secondary socialisation. A toddler watches a cartoon where a mouse hits a cat, and the toddler copies this behaviour, hitting the pet cat. The toddler cannot understand why this is wrong when he is only doing what he has seen **(c)**. The nursery may be the first place where a child meets people as agents of secondary socialisation. It is here that they may be interacting with others of the same age. Nursery nurses will teach them by showing them how to take turns, to care for others and to say 'please' and 'thank you'. At nursery or at home, children who are encouraged to become independent will find it easier to interact with others in the big wide world **(d)**.

Friends become agents of secondary socialisation in the teenage years, as they influence each other. Suddenly a certain type of trainer is fashionable and everyone must have one. Those who do not have them are seen as not belonging **(c)**.

Assessor report: The learner has defined socialisation and explained agents of primary socialisation but some of the work lacks depth. To achieve 2A.P1, the learner could improve their explanation of both positive and negative influences of the agents of primary and of secondary socialisation. To complete their work the learner should give both positive and negative examples of the influence for each type of socialisation. Agents of secondary socialisation require more explanation.

Assessor report – overall

What is good about this assessment evidence?

The learner has provided a definition of socialisation **(a)** and has explained the influence of agents of socialisation, both primary **(b)** and secondary **(c)**. They have said how the process happens and mentioned why **(d)**.

What could be improved about this assessment evidence?

In primary socialisation they should also look at the influence of agents on speech, beliefs and values. For secondary socialisation they should include friends and peers; media, e.g. advertising, social networking, television, celebrity culture, music, newspapers/magazines; and also other agents, e.g. early years workers at nursery/playgroup, teachers, youth workers, representatives of religions, work colleagues, social workers. They should span a wider age range and give more detail for the influence of agents of secondary socialisation.

2A.P2 Describe the effects of socialisation on the health and wellbeing of individuals.

Assessor report: The command verb in the grading criteria is **describe**. In the learner's answers we would expect to see a detailed account of the effects of socialisation on the health and wellbeing of individuals.

✍ Learner answer

Health, which is not just the absence of disease, and wellbeing, which is how we feel about ourselves, are influenced by how we are socialised. Socialisation can affect health and wellbeing both positively and negatively. In particular, socialisation can affect gender roles, attitudes, the development of social norms and values, and it can influence lifestyle choices.

Primary socialisation around gender roles can have a positive effect on health and wellbeing; for example, if a child is raised in a family where both mum and dad cook, change nappies, and clean the car, the child will develop a positive sense of wellbeing which will help them when they are in a relationship. They will be secure in their identity – a boy will not feel his masculinity is questioned because he changes a nappy and a girl will not be unhappy if both share parenting.

Primary socialisation can affect attitudes and can positively influence health and wellbeing. Children who are brought up to accept people from different cultures and religions will not be stressed living in a multicultural society, whereas those brought up to be prejudiced will be unhappy.

Primary socialisation affects the development of social norms and values positively. A child brought up to have good manners, to respect others and say 'please' and 'thank you' will be welcomed and will have a greater sense of wellbeing than one who is brought up to be selfish.

Lifestyle choices influence health and wellbeing. Primary socialisation can affect lifestyle choices positively, by developing a healthy lifestyle with a well-balanced diet and plenty of exercise, or it can have a negative influence on health and wellbeing. Parents who smoke, drink too much and take drugs are socialising their children in a way that will negatively affect their future health and wellbeing. A child who sees an adult they love smoking is more likely to start smoking to copy them, and is more likely to suffer the health problems associated with smoking such as asthma, lung disease and heart disease.

Secondary socialisation affects the health and wellbeing of individuals through gender roles, attitudes, the development of social norms and values and by influence on lifestyle choices. The effect may be positive or it may be negative.

Assessor report: The learner has made a good start in describing the effects of primary socialisation on health and wellbeing but needs to do the same for secondary socialisation.

Assessor report – overall

What is good about this assessment evidence?

The learner has given a detailed account of the effects of primary socialisation on gender roles, attitudes, the development of social norms and values and lifestyle choices.

What could be improved about this assessment evidence?

To achieve 2A.P2, the same detail is required for secondary socialisation and this should be applied to one or more fictional characters as set out in the scenario. Shaping of gender roles should include expectations for male and female behaviour. Shaping of attitudes should include the development of tolerance/prejudice, shaping of moral choices, religious and secular beliefs, and attitudes to authority. The development of social norms and values should include views of right and wrong, manners and behaviour and use of language. The effects of socialisation on lifestyle choices could include whether to enter employment, career choices, use of illegal substances, marriage and long-term relationships, alternative lifestyles, religion, use and choice of medical care and treatment, smoking, alcohol consumption and participation in sport or exercise.

2A.M1 Explain the effects of primary and secondary socialisation on the health and wellbeing of individuals, with reference to relevant examples.

Assessor report: The command verb in the grading criteria is **explain**. In the learner's answers we would expect to see that the learner has developed the points made for 2A.P2 and has provided more detail on the effects of primary and secondary socialisation with reference to relevant examples.

✍ Learner answer

Health, which is not just the absence of disease, and wellbeing, which is how we feel about ourselves, is influenced by how we are socialised, how we learn to interact with others. Socialisation can affect health and wellbeing both positively and negatively. In particular, socialisation can affect gender roles, attitudes, the development of social norms and values and it can influence lifestyle choices.

Primary socialisation around gender roles can have a positive effect on health and wellbeing; for example, if a child is raised in a family where both mum and dad cook, change nappies, and clean the car, the child will develop a positive sense of wellbeing which will help them when they are in a relationship. They will be secure in their identity – a boy will not feel his masculinity is questioned because he changes a nappy and a girl will not be unhappy if both share parenting.

Primary socialisation around gender can also have a negative impact on health and wellbeing. Jake was born into a family of travellers. It was a close-knit community and his grandparents were always close by. The men in his family were fighters and were taught never to run away from trouble but to stand and fight. The boys practised sparring. Girls were expected to know their place in the kitchen and not interfere. Jake did not really like to fight and felt sick at the sight of blood but could not let his father know so had to pretend to be tough. This caused Jake a lot of stress and negatively affected his wellbeing, as well as impacting on his health when he got a fractured nose in a fight **(a)**.

Primary socialisation can affect attitudes and can positively influence health and wellbeing. Children who are brought up to accept people from different cultures and religions will not be stressed living in a multicultural society, whereas those brought up to be prejudiced may be unhappy.

As travellers, the family experienced a lot of prejudice and rejection. Jake was brought up to believe that his family were always right and others were wrong. This made it difficult for him to accept outsiders. When he started school, his aggressive behaviour, learned from primary socialisation, starting fights got him into trouble **(a)**.

Primary socialisation affects the development of social norms and values positively. A child brought up to have good manners, to respect others and say 'please' and 'thank you' will be welcomed and will have a greater sense of wellbeing than one who is brought up to be selfish.

Lifestyle choices influence health and wellbeing. Primary socialisation can affect lifestyle choices positively, by developing a healthy lifestyle with a well balanced diet and plenty of exercise, or it can have a negative influence on health and wellbeing. Parents who smoke, drink too much and take drugs are socialising their children in a way that will negatively affect their future health and wellbeing. A child who sees an adult they love smoking is more likely to start smoking to copy them, and is more likely to suffer the health problems associated with smoking such as asthma, lung disease and heart disease.

Jake's father and uncles liked to drink. It was part of what they saw as 'being a man'. When they were drunk they would pick on an outsider and start a fight. Jake grew up to think that that is how all men behave. When his father was in hospital after being stabbed in a fight, Jake began to question the norms and values with which he had been raised **(a)**.

Secondary socialisation affects the health and wellbeing of individuals through gender roles, attitudes, the development of social norms and values and by influence on lifestyle choices. The effect may be positive or it may be negative.

Assessor report: The learner has made a good start in explaining the effects of primary socialisation on health and wellbeing with relevant examples, but needs to do the same for secondary socialisation.

Assessor report – overall

What is good about this assessment evidence?

The learner has given a detailed account of the effects of primary socialisation on gender roles, attitudes, the development of social norms and values and lifestyle choices. The learner has applied this to a relevant example, following an individual through primary socialisation (a).

What could be improved about this assessment evidence?

The same detail is required for secondary socialisation and this should be applied to more fictional characters as set out in the scenario. Shaping of attitudes should include the development of tolerance/prejudice, shaping of moral choices, religious and secular beliefs, and attitudes to authority. The development of social norms and values should include views of right and wrong, manners and behaviour and use of language. The effects of socialisation on lifestyle choices could include whether to enter employment, career choices, use of illegal substances, marriage and long-term relationships, alternative lifestyles, religion, use and choice of medical care and treatment, smoking, alcohol consumption and participation in sport or exercise. The learner should use further examples through the detail of secondary socialisation. They should be able to explain these effects, using either two detailed examples or a wider range of illustrative examples.

2A.D1 **Evaluate the impact of primary and secondary socialisation on the health and wellbeing of individuals, with reference to relevant examples.**

Assessor report: The command verb in the grading criteria is **evaluate**. Learners should cover all the information and form a judgement about the relative importance of these factors. They should support their argument with at least three detailed examples. They should decide which has most influence on the person studied, primary or secondary socialisation, and whether it had a largely positive or negative impact.

✍ Learner answer

Health, which is not just the absence of disease, and wellbeing, which is how we feel about ourselves, is influenced by how we learn to interact with others. Socialisation can affect health and wellbeing both positively and negatively. In particular socialisation can affect gender roles, attitudes, the development of social norms and values and it can influence lifestyle choices.

Primary socialisation around gender roles can have a positive effect on health and wellbeing; for example, a child raised in a family where both mum and dad change nappies and clean the car will be secure in their identity — a boy will not feel his masculinity is questioned because he changes a nappy and a girl will not be unhappy if both share parenting.

Primary socialisation around gender can also have a negative impact on health and wellbeing. Jake was born into a family of travellers. It was a close-knit community and his grandparents were always close by. The men in his family were fighters and were taught never to run away from trouble but to stand and fight. The boys practised sparring. Girls were expected to know their place in the kitchen and not interfere. Jake did not really like to fight and felt sick at the sight of blood but could not let his father know so had to pretend to be tough. This caused Jake a lot of stress and negatively affected his wellbeing, as well as impacting on his health when he got a fractured nose in a fight.

Primary socialisation affects attitudes and can positively or negatively influence health and wellbeing. Children who are brought up to accept people from different cultures and religions cope in a multicultural society, whereas those brought up to be prejudiced may be unhappy. As travellers, the family experienced prejudice and rejection. Jake was brought up to believe that his family were always right and others were wrong. This made it difficult for him to accept outsiders. When he started school starting fights, which earned praise at home, got him into trouble.

Primary socialisation can affect social norms and values positively. A child brought up to respect others and say 'please' and 'thank you' will be welcomed and will have a greater sense of wellbeing than one who is brought up to be aggressive.

Lifestyle choices influence health and wellbeing. Primary socialisation can affect lifestyle choices positively, by developing a healthy lifestyle with a well balanced diet and plenty of exercise, or it can have a negative influence on health and wellbeing. A child who sees parents smoking is more likely to copy them, and is more likely to suffer associated health problems such as asthma, lung and heart disease.

Jake's father and uncles liked to drink. It was part of what they saw as 'being a man'. When they were drunk they would pick on an outsider and start a fight. Jake grew up to think that that is how all men behave. When his father Mick was stabbed in a fight, Jake began to question the norms and values with which he had been raised.

So far we have seen that Jake's health and wellbeing is negatively influenced by his primary socialisation. Gender roles are strictly and narrowly defined in his family, and no variation is allowed so he cannot say that he does not like fighting. Attitudes are rigid – men and women have clearly defined roles which do not overlap. Social norms and values, to fight and to pick on an innocent victim, although acceptable in Jake's community, can lead him into trouble in the wider world. This can negatively affect his wellbeing. Lifestyle choices of fighting and drinking too much are risky behaviours in terms of health. Physical damage through fractures, a ruptured spleen or a damaged liver as a result of too much alcohol, are all negative influences on Jake's health and wellbeing **(a)**.

Secondary socialisation affects the health and wellbeing of individuals through gender roles, attitudes the development of social norms and values and by influence on lifestyle choices. The effect may be positive or it may be negative. Secondary socialisation may reinforce what has been learned in primary socialisation or it may challenge it.

Mick, Jake's father, and Tom, Jake's uncle, did not go to school and did not mix with people from outside their community.

Neither learned to read so they could not read books or newspapers, limiting their secondary socialisation. Mixing only with people like themselves reinforced their ideas of gender roles, attitudes about authority and their dislike of the police. This closed attitude narrowed their choice of lifestyle. They could not read so could not get steady employment. Because of their attitude to authority and their lack of a fixed address, neither had registered with a doctor and so they missed out on health checks. Leaflets about the dangers of smoking and alcohol were of no use to them (b).

Mick has been in prison several times for grievous bodily harm. Jake is afraid that one day his father will be killed in a fight. Tom nearly died when someone he attacked came back with a gang armed with machetes. Although Tom survived the fight, he suffers depression, because according to his norms, real men do not lose. He feels it is shameful not to seek revenge. For both Tom and Mick, their primary and their secondary socialisation have reinforced behaviours which negatively impact on their health and wellbeing but their primary socialisation seems to have been of most influence (b).

Jake, however, realised that to get on at school, he had to learn other ways of interacting. Secondary socialisation showed him that men do not have to fight. They can do other things. He learned about other people, their religions and festivals and that we can like people even though they are different from us. He really liked his teacher, Mrs Roberts, and did well at school, learning to read quickly. He realised that although he loved his family, especially his dad, there were other ways of behaving that were healthier. Later he turned his fighting skills into boxing skills, and became a junior champion. Secondary socialisation opened new opportunities. He got information to help his uncle through depression. In Jake's case, secondary socialisation has been a positive influence on his health and on his wellbeing. As a boxer, developing through school, he has to take care of his diet and exercise. He can legally practice the skills he learned rather than taking part in illegal fights. He can also help his family to a greater sense of wellbeing and better health (a). Tom and Mick both experience the negative influence of primary and secondary socialisation on their health and wellbeing, but Jake overcame the negative effects of his primary socialisation and through secondary socialisation achieved health and a greater sense of wellbeing, so overall for him, secondary socialisation was more important.

Assessor report: The learner has evaluated the impact of primary and secondary socialisation on the health and wellbeing of Jake **(a)** and to a lesser extent on Tom and Mick **(b)**.

Assessor report – overall

What is good about this assessment evidence?

The learner has given an account of the effects of primary socialisation on gender roles, attitudes, the development of social norms and values and lifestyle choices and has applied this to examples.

What could be improved about this assessment evidence?

A wider range of examples is required and a more detailed evaluation of the impact of secondary socialisation would strengthen this work. Social norms and values should include views of right and wrong, manners and behaviour and use of language. The effects of socialisation on lifestyle choices could include whether to enter employment, career choices, use of illegal substances, marriage and long-term relationships, alternative lifestyles, religion, use and choice of medical care and treatment, smoking, alcohol consumption, participation in sport or exercise. The learner should use further examples through the detail of secondary socialisation and discuss their relative impact. Learners should decide which factors have had most impact, and should support their conclusions with at least three detailed examples. Overall learners need to decide whether primary or secondary socialisation has had most influence. Alternatively they could decide whether factors have had a positive or a negative influence. The strongest essays will consider the impact of primary and of secondary socialisation and whether each was strongly positive or strongly negative, or whether they were balanced in their influence.

Learning aim B
Understand the influences that relationships have on the health and wellbeing of individuals

Assessment criteria

2B.P3   Describe the influences that different types of relationships have on the health and wellbeing of individuals.

2B.M2   Explain the influences that different types of relationships have on the health and wellbeing of individuals.

2B.D2   Compare the potential positive and negative influences of different relationships on the health and wellbeing of individuals.

Influences of relationships on individuals

Relationships influence an individual's health and wellbeing. When these relationships alter, for example, in marriage, divorce, bereavement and leaving education, these changes also have their impact on health and wellbeing. They affect our self-esteem, levels of stress and levels of anxiety. Dysfunctional relationships – ones that are not working well – also affect health and wellbeing.

Types of relationships

Different types of relationship include:

- family; for example, extended, nuclear, reconstituted, single-parent
- working; for example, teacher/student, colleagues, line managers
- social; for example, friends, fellow members of religious and secular groups
- intimate and sexual relationships.

Figure 2.1 Social relationships

Figure 2.2 Working relationships

Figure 2.3 Family relationships

Figure 2.4 Intimate relationships

The effect of family relationships

Studied ☐

Extended families include children, parents, grandparents, aunts, uncles and cousins. Nuclear families include just children and their parents. Reconstituted families may include children from different marriages, their parent and their step-parent when mum or dad remarry or have a new partner. Single-parent families consist of one parent, either mum or dad, and one or more children.

Children thrive in a secure loving family where they are loved. It does not matter what family type it is as long as they know they belong. A stable loving family has a positive influence on a child's health and wellbeing. When family relationships break down, parents are arguing or even violent, the family unit becomes unstable and a child feels insecure and uncertain of their place. They may feel unloved and may blame themselves for the break-up. This is stressful for the child, increases their anxiety and may damage their self-esteem as they feel they are no longer worthy of love. This dysfunctional family relationship has a negative impact on health and on wellbeing. A child might start bedwetting; a parent might drink too much and neglect themselves and the children.

Figure 2.5 Children will thrive in a secure loving family

The effect of working relationships

Relationships between teacher and student or between colleagues and line managers can influence health and wellbeing positively or negatively. A supportive and encouraging relationship encourages development and a positive self-esteem. A negative relationship where one person belittles and bullies another is destructive of self-esteem and harmful to health and wellbeing. Neither the bully nor the person being bullied function well.

Figure 2.6 Supportive relationships in the workplace

The effect of social relationships

Friends and fellow members of religious and secular groups can positively influence health and wellbeing. Belonging to a group and gaining respect boosts self-esteem and mental wellbeing. The harmful effects of loneliness and isolation are reduced. If, however, social relationships become harmful, by a group or a person exploiting another, this can cause stress and destroy self-esteem. The exploited person may suffer anxiety, feel depressed, have disturbed sleep patterns and gain or lose weight.

Figure 2.7 Being part of a religious group can positively influence health and wellbeing

UNIT 4 Social Influences on Health and Wellbeing

The effect of intimate and sexual relationships

Intimate, close relationships, whether sex is involved or not, can benefit individuals if the relationship is equal and there is mutual respect. They support each other through hard times and care for each other's welfare. Even though they may have illnesses, they have a positive sense of wellbeing. You can see this where older people who have been married for a very long time care for each other. When ones dies, often the other person dies because they no longer have that positive sustaining relationship.

When intimate relationships are not mutually respectful, they can destroy health and wellbeing. A relationship where one partner abuses another is not mutually respectful. The abused person loses self-esteem, is unhappy, depressed and can become mentally and physically unwell. Where there is physical abuse, the victim may have broken bones; where there is mental abuse, the victim may feel worthless and suicidal.

Knowledge recap questions

1. There are four types of relationship in this section. What are they?

2. What is a reconstituted family?

3. Explain how the breakdown of a family relationship may affect a child's health and wellbeing.

4. A relationship where both people care for each other is an example of a positive/ negative (choose one) influence on health and wellbeing.

5. A member of staff is being bullied by their boss. Describe the effect this could have on the member of staff's health and wellbeing.

Learning aim B: Understand the influences that relationships have on the health and wellbeing of individuals

Assessment guidance for learning aim B

(2B.P3) **Describe the influences that different types of relationships have on the health and wellbeing of individuals.**

Assessor report: The command verb in the grading criteria is **describe**. In the learner's answers we would expect to see a detailed account of the influences that different types of relationships have on the health and wellbeing of individuals.

✍️ Learner answer

Relationships are the bonds that are built between people. There are many different types of relationships but here we will look at just four: family relationships, working relationships, social relationships and intimate or sexual relationships. Each type of relationship can influence our physical and mental health and can influence our wellbeing – how we feel about ourselves.

Family relationships have a big impact on our health and how we feel about ourselves. If parents neglect a child by not feeding them a balanced diet, the child may not grow well. If parents do not love the child and talk to him, he may be late learning to speak.

If a child is always told they are no good, their self-esteem will be low.

Working relationships influence health and wellbeing. A person who has a good relationship with their teachers and knows they can ask if they need help will feel confident and good about their work. They may not be the best student but they will do their best as they are encouraged. A person who has a bully for a teacher will not feel confident to ask, and may feel bad about themselves thinking that they must be stupid if they do not understand.

Assessor report: The learner has made a good start in describing the influences that different types of relationships have on the health and wellbeing of individuals.

Assessor report – overall

What is good about this assessment evidence?

The learner has described the positive and negative influence of family relationships and working relationships.

What could be improved about this assessment evidence?

All four types of relationship should be described and their potential positive and negative effects. Family relationships should be described in more detail to reflect the different types of family, for example, extended, nuclear, reconstituted and single-parent.

Explain the influences that different types of relationships have on the health and wellbeing of individuals.

Assessor report: The command verb in the grading criteria is **explain**. In the learner's answers we would expect to see details and reasons and/or evidence to support the arguments being made. The learner should start by introducing the topic then give the 'how' or 'why'.

✍ Learner answer

Relationships are the bonds that are built between people. There are many different types of relationships but here we will look at just four: family relationships, working relationships, social relationships and intimate or sexual relationships. Each type of relationship can influence our physical and mental health and can influence our wellbeing – how we feel about ourselves.

How relationships influence our health and our wellbeing is not fully understood, but it is known that stress can cause physical symptoms, for example, chest pain or even heart attacks, or it can cause problems such as colitis. Stress can cause eating disorders. Some people drink or smoke too much and then get health problems such as liver disease or lung disease. These are negative influences **(a)**.

Relationships can influence health and wellbeing positively too. A child raised in a loving family where they are valued will feel good about themselves. A person working in a positive environment where a boss appreciates what they do will be less likely to take time off sick. A couple in a relationship where there is mutual love and respect are likely to stay healthier and have a better sense of wellbeing than a person on their own **(a)**.

Family relationships have a big impact on our health and how we feel about ourselves. If parents neglect a child by not feeding them a balanced diet, the child may not grow well. If parents do not love the child and talk to him, he may be late learning to speak **(a)**.

If a child is always told they are no good, their self-esteem will be low.

Families come in all shapes and sizes. Extended families include grandparents, aunts and uncles as well as parents **(b)**. A child in an extended family is likely to have a strong sense of belonging and someone around all the time to care for them **(c)**.

In a nuclear or single-parent family **(b)** with no relatives nearby, there is less support and a child could feel more isolated especially if the parents have to work **(c)**.

A reconstituted family **(b)**, where there may be children from different marriages, can influence health and wellbeing. A child whose own parents have split up may have experienced stress. To then have a new parent figure and other children in the home may cause more stress. As we have seen, stress can affect health. A child who is stressed may start to wet the bed or have nightmares. Suddenly they are no longer sure of their place in the family and they may become withdrawn. The influence of the family changes how they feel about themselves, and changes their wellbeing **(c)**.

Working relationships influence health and wellbeing. A person who has a good relationship with their teachers and knows they can ask if they need help will feel confident and good about their work. They may not be the best student but they will do their best as they are encouraged. A person who has a bully for a teacher will not feel confident to ask, and may feel bad about themselves thinking that they must be stupid if they do not understand.

Assessor report: The learner has explained in detail how relationships can influence our health and wellbeing and has explained some of the negative influences of some family relationships on the health and wellbeing of individuals.

Assessor report – overall

What is good about this assessment evidence?

The learner introduced the topic and then explained the 'link' between relationships and health and wellbeing **(a)**. They give more detail about family types **(b)** and explain the link between family types and health and wellbeing **(c)**.

What could be improved about this assessment evidence?

A balance of positive and negative influences should be explained for each type of relationship.

The other types of relationship, social and intimate or sexual relationships, also need to be included.

Compare the potential positive and negative influences of different relationships on the health and wellbeing of individuals.

Assessor report: The command verb in the grading criteria is **compare**. In the learner's answer we would expect to see examples of potential positive and potential negative influences on health and wellbeing compared and contrasted.

✍️ **Learner answer**

Relationships are the bonds that are built between people. There are many different types of relationships but here we will look at just four: family relationships, working relationships, social relationships and intimate or sexual relationships. Each type of relationship can influence our physical and mental health and can influence our wellbeing – how we feel about ourselves.

How relationships influence our health and our wellbeing is not fully understood, but it is known that stress can cause physical symptoms such as chest pain or even heart attacks, or it can cause problems such as colitis. Stress can cause eating disorders. Some people drink or smoke too much and then get health problems such as liver disease or lung disease. These are negative influences.

Relationships can influence health and wellbeing positively too. A child raised in a loving family where they are valued will feel good about themselves. A person working in a positive environment where a boss appreciates what they do will be less likely to take time off sick. A couple in a relationship where there is mutual love and respect are likely to stay healthier and have a better sense of wellbeing than a person on their own.

Family relationships have a big impact on our health and how we feel about ourselves and this impact may last throughout our lives. Families come in all shapes and sizes. Extended families include grandparents, aunts and uncles as well as parents. A child in an extended family is likely to have a strong sense of belonging and someone around all the time to care for them **(a)**. This may be a positive influence as they develop confidence and a positive self-esteem. It can, however, become a negative influence as a child grows.

Sameerah grew up in a Pakistani family in Bradford. She had a strong sense of belonging, surrounded by aunties and uncles **(a)**, brothers, sisters and cousins. When she was twelve she decided she wanted to become a doctor. Her family were happy with this but when she reached seventeen they decided she should marry. She had to miss classes while she was abroad getting married, and then her new husband decided he did not want her to become a doctor, he wanted her to be a housewife and her parents supported him. For the first time, Sameerah felt the negative pressure of an extended family **(b)**. The stress made her ill. She gave up her ambition as she could not cope with the stress of going against her family. In this example we see that extended families can have a positive influence on health and wellbeing but can also have a negative effect too.

It would be easy to contrast different types of family relationship and say one type of family is better than another, but it would not be true. Nuclear families can have a positive influence or can have a negative influence **(c)**. Ben, a two-year-old, grew up in a nuclear family. His parents were both drug addicts and he would be left in a room on his own when they were spaced out. A neighbour reported the family. The social worker found Ben in a cot, chewing a crust of bread, with a nappy that had not been changed for days. His bottom was covered in sores and he had bruises where he had either been beaten or had fallen. He was taken into care. This nuclear family negatively influenced Ben's health **(b)**. In contrast, Jake, also a two-year-old, lived with his mum and dad. His dad was an electrician and his mum worked part-time two evenings a week, when Jake's dad looked after him. This nuclear family provided a positive influence on Jake **(a)**. He had people who loved and cared for him, thus developing his sense of wellbeing. He was cared for and fed, and apart from the usual coughs and colds had perfect health.

Both examples of nuclear families show the potential for positive and for negative influences on health and on wellbeing **(c)**.

In a single-parent family with no relatives nearby, there is less support and a child could feel more isolated especially if the parent has to work **(b)**. This can have a negative effect on wellbeing as the child may grow up lonely. If, however, the parent is able to tap into a network of similar one-parent families, the child will learn to mix with others **(a)**. If the parent can move to be near relatives, they can provide support when the parent is working and the child will not be so isolated.

A reconstituted family, where there may be children from different marriages, can influence health and wellbeing. A child whose own parents have split up may have experienced stress.

To then have a new parent figure and other children in the home may cause more stress. As we have seen, stress can affect health. A child who is stressed may start to wet the bed or have nightmares. Suddenly they are no longer sure of their place in the family and they may become withdrawn. The influence of the family negatively changes how they feel about themselves, and changes their wellbeing **(b)**.

Not all children in reconstituted families feel this stress. If parents communicate and explain what is happening, a child may find it easier to accept that both parents still love him even though they are not together. If they are included in decisions that affect them, they may find it easier to adjust and the reconstituted family may have a less negative effect on their health and wellbeing. If they feel loved and valued, their sense of wellbeing is likely to be stronger than if they are not included. They may benefit from having more family members to care for them and to care for **(a)**.

Working relationships influence health and wellbeing. A person who has a good relationship with their teachers and knows they can ask if they need help will feel confident and good about their work **(a)**. They may not be the best student but they will do their best as they are encouraged. A person who has a bully for a teacher will not feel confident to ask, and may feel bad about themselves thinking that they must be stupid if they do not understand **(b)**.

Assessor report: The learner has explained in detail how relationships can influence our health and wellbeing and has compared some of the potential positive **(a)** and negative influences **(b)** of some family relationships – a good start to this section.

Assessor report – overall

What is good about this assessment evidence?

The learner compares and contrasts the link between family types and health and wellbeing **(c)**.

What could be improved about this assessment evidence?

The influence of remaining types of relationship (working, social and intimate and sexual relationships) should also be compared and contrasted.

Learning aim C

Investigate the effects of social factors on the health and wellbeing of individuals

Assessment criteria

2C.P4	Describe how social factors can affect the health and wellbeing of individuals.
2C.M3	Explain how social factors can affect the health and wellbeing of individuals, with reference to relevant examples.
2C.D3	Evaluate the link between social factors and the health and wellbeing of individuals, and the impact on health and wellbeing, with reference to relevant examples.

How social factors influence health and wellbeing

Social factors that influence health and wellbeing

Studied ☐

Health is more than being free from physical illness. Physical, intellectual, emotional and social wellbeing are aspects of health and wellbeing. Social factors that influence health and wellbeing include:

Income, education, occupation and social class

Income, or how much money comes into a household, dictates whether a person can afford a holiday, what food they can buy, and whether they can afford heating in cold weather. Income, education, occupation and social class are often linked together in the way they influence health and wellbeing.

A person's level of education affects what occupation or job they can get and their job and income affect their social class. People working in professional and managerial occupations, such as doctors and lawyers, have a higher social class than those in unskilled occupations such as labourers. Higher social classes earn more, enjoy better health and, according to research, their children do better at school than those from lower social classes. Manual work carries higher risks. In 2010 more people died from work-related injuries in the construction industry than in any other occupation.

Wealth

Wealth is the amount of money and possessions a person has including savings and income. A person who is wealthy can afford private healthcare when they need it. Those who cannot afford private care join the NHS waiting list.

Values and behaviours

Values and behaviours influence what we do. Some people take responsibility for their own health, eating and drinking in moderation, and taking exercise. Other people think the NHS will be able to cure them if they drink too much or become obese. Their values are that it is someone else's responsibility to make them better and this influences their health.

Family

Families influence health and wellbeing as we saw in section B. They can be a positive resource, supporting individuals to develop a strong sense of wellbeing, or they can negatively influence a person's health.

Peers

Peers influence health and wellbeing. Peers can be a positive influence, for example, friends may play sport together, or they can be a negative influence, encouraging each other to drink too much or take drugs.

Figure 3.1 Playing sport with friends can be a positive influence on health and wellbeing

Media

The media, social networking, the internet, television, and teen magazines may focus on body image, influencing many young people with low self-esteem to diet and at times become anorexic. Facebook and Twitter increasingly influence health and wellbeing.

Living conditions

Living conditions influence health and wellbeing. Living in an overcrowded and damp flat with no garden will restrict how much a child can play outside. Damp and mould may cause asthma. Living with people who smoke will negatively impact on a child's health, as they breathe in the smoke.

Gender

Gender affects health and wellbeing. According to government statistics, women born in the UK between 2008 and 2010 can expect to live on average until they are 82, but men can expect to live only until they are 78.

Culture

Culture affects whether people care for each other. Individuals in contact with family and friends may have a greater sense of wellbeing than someone who is isolated. In a culture where people do not care for each other, children and the elderly are neglected and health suffers. Old people may die of hypothermia; children may starve. America, one of the richest countries in the world, does not provide healthcare for all. Lack of healthcare has a negative effect both on their wellbeing and on their health.

When factors come together negatively, for example low income, poor education and no job, they can reduce a person's sense of wellbeing and badly affect their health. On the other hand when they come together positively, for example, a high income, good education and a rewarding job, they can lead to better health and a greater sense of wellbeing. The effects may be long term or they may be short term.

Figure 3.2 Someone who is isolated may not have as great a sense of wellbeing

Effects of social factors on health choices

Social factors affect choices about:

- diet
- smoking
- living accommodation
- use of recreational drugs
- alcohol consumption
- participation in sport or exercise
- seeking medical care.

Diet is influenced by culture and family. For religious reasons, some families do not eat meat. Others do not eat pork, while others do not eat beef. A single person may eat out in restaurants or eat takeaway food because they have the income to do so, and do not want to bother with cooking.

Figure 3.3 Diet can be affected by social factors

Income decides what type of living accommodation we have, whether it is a council-owned property or we own our own home. Some people are forced to move in with relatives as they cannot afford a separate home, and this can lead to overcrowding. Tuberculosis is increasing as more families live in overcrowded living conditions.

Some people start smoking, drinking alcohol, or using drugs to fit in with friends. These choices then may be difficult to give up as they become addicted.

Figure 3.4 People start drinking to fit in with friends

Whether we take part in sport is often linked to income and occupation. A person with spare time and money may join a tennis club. Someone working long hours on a low wage may have neither the time nor the income to make such a choice.

Whether we seek medical care is influenced by how much time and money we have. A busy working man may not have time to have a check-up. A mother of a large family may not be able to afford to have dental treatment. Some older people are reluctant to seek medical advice because they do not want to be a nuisance. Homeless people have very little chance to seek medical care as they cannot register with a doctor.

Effects of social factors on health and wellbeing

Social factors affect:

- self-esteem
- levels of stress and anxiety
- access to health and social care services
- physical health.

Self-esteem, levels of stress and anxiety, access to health and social care services, all contribute to how happy we are, to our sense of wellbeing. Recent research found that women tend to be happier than men. It also found that having leisure time and being in a steady relationship all have positive effects on wellbeing. Both 16–19 and 65–69-year-olds are happier than middle-aged people. The highest sense of wellbeing was among the professional classes, higher earners and those with an occupation.

Figure 3.5 People aged 16–19/65–69 are happier

Self-esteem is greater if we have freedom to choose. Income and education influence how much choice we can have and therefore they influence our self-esteem. An individual with no money and poor education is likely to have less choice than one who has these things. Their self-esteem is likely to be lower if they have to ask others for help with food and somewhere to live.

Levels of stress and anxiety are influenced by values and behaviour. Someone who cares about others and knows their behaviour impacts on other people is likely to be more stressed than someone who cares only for themselves. A man who is made redundant may feel acute anxiety about how he is to provide for his family now he has lost his job. This is because he sees himself as the provider for the family. It is part of his values.

Access to health and social care services is not always free, so income is a factor. Dentists and opticians charge adults, so a parent on a low income may not go to the dentist until they have problems, whereas someone with a high income can afford regular check-ups.

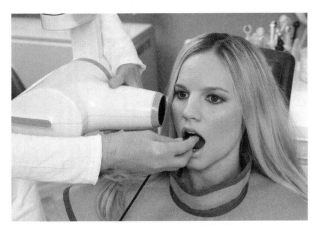

Figure 3.6 Adults are charged to visit the dentist and optician

Physical health, as we saw earlier, is affected by values and behaviour. A person who smokes, drinks and eats a diet of chips and burgers will be more likely to develop heart disease, lung cancer and liver disease than someone who does not make these choices.

Knowledge recap questions

1. Name twelve social factors that influence health and wellbeing.

2. How might social factors affect health choices?

3. How might social factors affect health and wellbeing?

Assessment guidance for learning aim C

Scenario

At a local youth club, the organisers want young people to understand the influences that social factors have on the health and wellbeing of individuals. They have asked you to prepare a set of resources to show this.

· ·

2C.P4 **Describe how social factors can affect the health and wellbeing of individuals.**

· ·

Assessor report: The command verb in the grading criteria is **describe**. In the learner's answers we would expect to see a detailed account of how social factors can affect the health and wellbeing of individuals. Learners should describe at least four factors and their effects on health and wellbeing.

✍ **Learner answer**

There are many social factors that influence health and wellbeing. These include income, education, occupation, social class, wealth, values and behaviours, family, peers, media, living conditions, gender and culture **(a)**.

Income is how much money we have coming in. If we have a lot of income we can choose what food we eat, where we live and how we spend our spare time. If we wish we can eat plenty of fruit and vegetables, live in a nice area with a large house and garden, and we can spend time at the gym. If we do not have much money, we cannot have as much choice about what types of food we eat. We may have to eat cheaper food and cut out expensive fruit and vegetables. We may have to rely on the council to provide us with a place to live, and rely on housing benefit to pay for it. We then have little choice about where we live or what type of place we live in. We do not have money to go to the gym or buy the clothes and equipment we need to keep fit. We may just sit at home watching television, eating chips and getting fat **(b)**.

Peers have a big influence on our wellbeing. Sometimes we do things to fit in, even if we do not like them. We may try smoking or drugs because our friends do it and we want to be like them. Sometimes peers introduce us to healthy lifestyles, for example, a group of friends may run a marathon together for charity. Training and running a marathon makes us physically fit and we also get a sense of wellbeing by doing things with our friends and doing things for charity (c).

Assessor report: The learner has explained in detail how one social factor (income) can influence our health and wellbeing (b). They have also begun to describe how our peers can influence our health and wellbeing – a good start to this section (c).

Assessor report – overall

What is good about this assessment evidence?

The learner lists all the social factors that can affect health and wellbeing (a) and then gives a detailed account of how income can affect the health and wellbeing of individuals (b).

What could be improved about this assessment evidence?

It would be good to have an introduction outlining briefly what is meant by health and wellbeing. To achieve 2C.P4, at least four factors should be described in detail. The learner has currently only described one (income) in detail and one (peers) briefly. The learner needs to include a similar level of detail as they have provided for income for three other social factors.

2C.M3 **Explain how social factors can affect the health and wellbeing of individuals, with reference to relevant examples.**

Assessor report: The command verb in the grading criteria is **explain**. In the learner's answers we would expect to see details and reasons and/or evidence to support the arguments being made. The learner should start by introducing the topic then give the 'how' or 'why' using relevant examples to support their arguments. They should explain the wider effects of these social factors on the overall health and wellbeing of people and should give a detailed example of the effects for each social factor.

✍ Learner answer

Health is not just the absence of disease but is also having a positive sense of wellbeing. Health is more than physical health. It includes social, emotional and intellectual wellbeing too **(a)**. We have seen how families influence health and wellbeing. Now we look at social factors that influence health and wellbeing. These include income, education, occupation, social class, wealth, values and behaviours, family, peers, media, living conditions, gender and culture **(b)**.

Income is how much money we have coming in. It can influence our physical, social, emotional and intellectual health and wellbeing. If we have a lot of income we can choose what food we eat, and we can choose healthy food such as fruit and vegetables to give us vitamins and minerals. Milk and meat give protein for strong bones and teeth. With a good income we can live in a nice area with a large house and garden, and we can spend time at the gym. We gain socially by meeting people, emotionally by having a positive sense of wellbeing, and intellectually by learning new skills.

If we do not have much money, we cannot have as much choice about what types of food we eat. We may have to eat cheaper food and cut out expensive fruit and vegetables. A diet that is heavy in carbohydrates such as bread, chips and pizza, leads to obesity and a lack of fruit and vegetables leads to vitamin deficiency. Our physical health is then poor. If we are obese we tend not to exercise and our physical health suffers. We may develop heart disease, or have a stroke. If we do not have much income, we may have to rely on the council to provide us with a place to live, and rely on housing benefit to pay for it. We then have little choice about where we live or what type of place we live in. We do not have money to go to the gym or buy the clothes and equipment we need to keep fit. We may just sit at home watching television, eating chips and getting fat. We then have less chance to socialise, to learn new skills and emotionally may feel depressed. One of the best ways to overcome depression is exercise, but an obese person with poor self-esteem is less likely to exercise, and they become trapped in a cycle of comfort eating to make them good, which leads to more weight problems.

Income affects health and wellbeing. Jack is on an apprenticeship scheme learning to be a plumber. He has a steady income from a part-time job too. He can afford to go out with his friends, but he limits what he drinks as he has to drive home. He plays football at the weekend. Physically, socially, emotionally and intellectually he is healthy and he has a positive sense of wellbeing **(c)**. Russ, his school friend, is unemployed and not at college. He has no money to go out with friends, so stays home watching television or playing computer games. He doesn't get out and is getting fat. Physically, socially and emotionally his health is poor. Intellectually he is not developing. His sense of wellbeing is poor. He is unhealthy because his income limits his choices **(c)**.

Peers have a big influence on our wellbeing, physically, socially, emotionally and intellectually. Sometimes we do things to fit in, even if we do not like them. We may try smoking or drugs because our friends do it and we want to be like them. Jack has a healthy sense of wellbeing. His self-esteem is high and emotionally he is able to say no to too much alcohol. He has other aspects to his life and does not need to risk his health to fit in **(c)**. Russ on the other hand may be greatly influenced by his mates as he has no other ways to gain a sense of wellbeing. When he can borrow enough from his mum to go out, he may drink too much to gain the approval of peers, thus risking his own physical health **(c)**. Sometimes peers introduce us to healthy lifestyles, for example, a group of friends may run a marathon together for charity. Training and running a marathon makes us physically fit and we also get a sense of wellbeing by doing things with our friends and doing things for charity. If Russ could join such a group his health would benefit physically, socially, emotionally and intellectually and his sense of wellbeing would be greater.

Assessor report: The learner has explained in detail how two social factors can influence our health and wellbeing and has given examples – a good start to this section.

Assessor report – overall

What is good about this assessment evidence?

The learner has included an introduction outlining what is meant by health and wellbeing **(a)**. They list all the social factors at the start **(b)** and then give a detailed account of how income and peers can affect the health and wellbeing of individuals. The learner includes examples which link to the scenario and support the argument **(c)**.

What could be improved about this assessment evidence?

The learner should complete their answer by explaining two further factors listed in their introduction in a similar level of detail. They should explain the wider effects of these social factors on the overall health and wellbeing of people and should give a detailed example of the effects for each social factor.

2C.D3 **Evaluate the link between social factors and the health and wellbeing of individuals, and the impact on health and wellbeing, with reference to relevant examples.**

Assessor report: The command verb in the grading criteria is **evaluate**. Learners should cover all the information and form a judgement about the relative importance of these factors. They should evaluate the link between social factors and evaluate the overall impact on the physical, intellectual, emotional and social wellbeing, not just their physical health or social wellbeing. A comprehensive assessment of these four areas is required.

✍ **Learner answer**

Health is not just the absence of disease but is also having a positive sense of wellbeing. Health is more than physical health. It includes social, emotional and intellectual wellbeing too. Social factors that influence health and wellbeing include income, education, occupation, social class, wealth, values and behaviours, family, peers, media, living conditions, gender and culture. Each of these factors influences physical, social, emotional and intellectual wellbeing. This essay will evaluate the link between these factors and physical, social, emotional and intellectual health and wellbeing.

Income, how much money we have coming in, influences our physical, social, emotional and intellectual health and wellbeing. If we have a lot of income we can choose what food we eat, and we can choose healthy food, such as fruit and vegetables to give us vitamins and minerals. Milk and meat give protein for strong bones and teeth. With a good income we can live in a nice area with a large house and garden, and we can spend time at the gym. We gain socially by meeting people, emotionally by having a positive sense of wellbeing, and intellectually learning new skills.

If we do not have much money, we cannot have as much choice what types of food we eat. We may have to eat cheaper food and cut out expensive fruit and vegetables. A diet that is heavy in carbohydrates such as bread, chips and pizza, leads to obesity and a lack of fruit and vegetables leads to vitamin deficiency. Our physical health is then poor. If we are obese we tend not to exercise and our physical health suffers. We may develop heart disease, or have a stroke. If we do not have much income, we may have to rely on the council to provide us with a place to live, and rely on housing benefit to pay for it. We then have little choice about where we live or what type of place we live in. We do not have money to go to the gym or buy the clothes and equipment we need to keep fit. We may just sit at home watching television, eating chips and getting fat. We then have less chance to socialise, to learn new skills and emotionally may feel depressed. One of the best ways to overcome depression is exercise, but an obese person with poor self-esteem is less likely to exercise, and they become trapped in a cycle of comfort eating to make them good, which leads to more weight problems.

Income affects health and wellbeing. Jack is learning to be a plumber. He has a steady income from a part-time job too. He can afford to go out with his friends, but he limits what he drinks as he has to drive home. He plays football at the weekend. Physically, socially, emotionally and intellectually, he is healthy and he has a positive sense of wellbeing. Russ, his school friend, is unemployed and not at college. He has no money to go out with friends, stays home watching television or playing computer games. He doesn't get out and is getting fat. Physically, socially and emotionally his health is poor. Intellectually he is not developing. His sense of wellbeing is poor. He is unhealthy because his income limits his choices. It would seem then that income has a major impact on physical health which then affects our social, emotional and intellectual wellbeing.

Peers have a big influence on our wellbeing, physically, socially, emotionally and intellectually but here the main influence is on our social wellbeing, which then affects our emotional wellbeing and can affect our physical health. Sometimes we do things to fit in, even if we do not like them. We may try smoking or drugs because our friends do it and we want to be like them. Jack has a healthy sense of wellbeing. His self-esteem is high and emotionally he is able to say no to too much alcohol. He has other aspects to his life and does not need to risk his health to fit in. Russ on the other hand may be greatly influenced by his mates as he has no other ways to gain a sense of wellbeing. When he can borrow enough from his mum to go out, he may drink too much to gain the approval of peers, thus risking his own physical health, but gaining social wellbeing. Sometimes peers introduce us to healthy lifestyles, for example, a group of friends may run a marathon together for charity. Training and running a marathon makes us physically fit and we also get a sense of wellbeing by doing things with our friends and doing things for charity. If Russ could join such a group his health would benefit physically, socially, emotionally and intellectually and his sense of wellbeing would be greater.

Education is an important social factor in early life. We may be physically healthy but if we do not do well in class we may suffer emotionally and intellectually. We may feel isolated if our friends achieve and we do not. This social, emotional and intellectual ill health can lead to physical ill health as a young person gets stressed and anxious. They may develop anxiety related eating disorders such as anorexia or bulimia. Jack's sister is at school and finds it hard to read. This slows her down and at times she does not understand the lessons. She gets stressed and often misses school. She feels socially isolated, emotionally she is unhappy and intellectually she has no confidence in her own abilities. Education impacts largely on intellectual, social and emotional wellbeing.

Education links closely to occupation and social class. Both occupation and social class impact on our sense of wellbeing. If we are in a job we like, can do well and feel proud to do, we have a greater sense of wellbeing. Social class is measured by occupation. Some occupations are rewarding but may also be risky to health. The construction industry has the greatest number of accidents, posing a greater risk to physical health than office work.

In conclusion, physical, intellectual, emotional and social wellbeing is influenced by social factors. Perhaps income has the greatest influence on physical health, peer pressure on social wellbeing, and education on intellectual wellbeing, but all the factors impact on all aspects of health in some way or another.

Assessor report: The learner has evaluated how three social factors can influence our health and wellbeing and has given examples – a good start to this section.

Assessor report – overall

What is good about this assessment evidence?

The learner has an introduction unpacking what is meant by health and wellbeing, gives all the social factors at the start and then gives a detailed account of how income, peers and education can affect the health and wellbeing of individuals. The learner includes examples which link to the scenario and support the argument and evaluates the impact of each on the four aspects of health.

What could be improved about this assessment evidence?

The learner should cover all the information and form a judgement about the relative importance of these factors. They should continue to evaluate the link between social factors and evaluate the overall impact on the physical, intellectual, emotional and social wellbeing, not just their physical health or social wellbeing. A comprehensive assessment of these four areas is required once all factors have been evaluated.

Sample assignment brief 1: The impact of socialisation on health and wellbeing

PROGRAMME NAME	BTEC Level 2 First Award in Health and Social Care
ASSIGNMENT TITLE	The impact of socialisation on health and wellbeing
ASSESSMENT EVIDENCE	Written report

This assignment will assess the following learning aim and grading criteria:

Learning Aim A: Explore the effects of socialisation on the health and wellbeing of individuals

(2A.P1) Explain the influence of agents of primary and secondary socialisation.

(2A.P2) Describe the effects of socialisation on the health and wellbeing of individuals.

(**2A.M1**) Explain the effects of primary and secondary socialisation on the health and wellbeing of individuals, with reference to relevant examples.

(2A.D1) Evaluate the impact of primary and secondary socialisation on the health and wellbeing of individuals, with reference to relevant examples.

Scenario

You are helping at a local youth club and the organisers want young people to be aware of the effect of socialisation on health and wellbeing. They have asked you to write short stories based on fictional characters to show this. Your work will need to explore the effects of socialisation on the health and wellbeing of individuals.

a) Say what we mean by 'agents of socialisation'. Give details of both primary and secondary socialisation, explaining the difference between them.

b) Give a detailed account of the effects of socialisation on the health and wellbeing of individuals.

c) Develop the points made in part b) and give details on the effects of primary and secondary socialisation, with reference to relevant examples or case studies which would have relevance to people attending a youth club as described in the scenario.

d) Form a judgement about the relative importance of these factors. Support your argument with at least three detailed examples. Decide which has most influence on the people studied, primary or secondary socialisation, and whether it had a largely positive or negative impact.

Sample assignment brief 2: The influences that relationships have on the health and wellbeing of individuals

PROGRAMME NAME	BTEC Level 2 First Award in Health and Social Care
ASSIGNMENT TITLE	The influences that relationships have on the health and wellbeing of individuals
ASSESSMENT EVIDENCE	Individual or small-group PowerPoint presentations, written reports, leaflets or handbooks

This assignment will assess the following learning aim and grading criteria:

Learning Aim B: Understand the influences that relationships have on the health and wellbeing of individuals

2B.P3   Describe the influences that different types of relationships have on the health and wellbeing of individuals.

2B.M2   Explain the influences that different types of relationships have on the health and wellbeing of individuals.

2B.D2   Compare the potential positive and negative influences of different relationships on the health and wellbeing of individuals.

Scenario

At a local youth club, the organisers want young people to understand the influences that relationships have on the health and wellbeing of individuals. They have asked you to prepare a set of resources to show which could be in the form of a leaflet or a handbook.

Task 1

a) Describe all four types of relationship – family, working, social, intimate or sexual relationships – and their potential positive and negative effects. Family relationships should be described in detail to reflect the different types of family, for example, extended, nuclear, reconstituted and single-parent.

b) Build on your work for part a) by giving details and reasons and/or evidence to support the arguments being made. Start by introducing the topic then give the 'how' or 'why'. Link this to examples or case studies that have relevance to people at a youth club.

c) Compare and contrast examples of potential positive and potential negative influences on health and wellbeing, using case studies to illustrate your arguments. Include all four types of relationship: family, working, social and intimate or sexual relationships.

This task should be presented as a series of case studies which can be added to your information pack.

Sample assignment brief 3: The effects of social factors on the health and wellbeing of individuals

PROGRAMME NAME	BTEC Level 2 First Award in Health and Social Care
ASSIGNMENT TITLE	The effects of social factors on the health and wellbeing of individuals
ASSESSMENT EVIDENCE	Individual or small-group PowerPoint presentations, written reports, leaflets or handbooks

This assignment will assess the following learning aim and grading criteria:

Learning Aim C: Investigate the effects of social factors on the health and wellbeing of individuals

- **2C.P4** Describe how social factors can affect the health and wellbeing of individuals.

- **2C.M3** Explain how social factors can affect the health and wellbeing of individuals, with reference to relevant examples.

- **2C.D3** Evaluate the link between social factors and the health and wellbeing of individuals, and the impact on health and wellbeing, with reference to relevant examples.

Scenario

At a local youth club, the organisers want young people to understand the influences that social factors have on the health and wellbeing of individuals. They have asked you to prepare a set of resources to show this. You may wish to make a PowerPoint presentation, or a handbook, to show them how social factors can impact on four aspects of health and wellbeing.

Task 1

a) Describe twelve different social factors that can affect health and four aspects of health and wellbeing that may be affected by these factors.

b) Give details and reasons and/or evidence to support the arguments being made. Start by introducing the topic or build on what you have already done for part a), then give the 'how' or 'why' using relevant examples to support your arguments. Explain the wider effects of these social factors on the overall health and wellbeing of people and give a detailed example of the effects for each social factor. Use examples that are relevant to young people.

c) Some factors have a greater influence than others. Remember this influence can be positive or it can be negative. Cover all the information and form a judgement about the relative importance of these factors. Evaluate the link between social factors, saying which factors have most influence and which have least. Factors may have a great influence or little influence. They may have a positive influence or a negative influence. Bringing these together, a factor may have a large negative impact, or a large positive impact, a small negative impact or a small positive impact. Remember to support what you say with evidence.

You will need to evaluate the overall impact on the physical, intellectual, emotional and social wellbeing, of your case studies, not just on their physical health or social wellbeing. A comprehensive assessment of these four areas is required. Again remember to make the point and support it with an example or evidence.

Assessment criteria

Level 2 Pass	Level 2 Merit	Level 2 Distinction
Learning Aim A: Explore the effects of socialisation on the health and wellbeing of individuals		
2A.P1 Explain the influence of agents of primary and secondary socialisation.	**2A.M1** Explain the effects of primary and secondary socialisation on the health and wellbeing of individuals, with reference to relevant examples.	**2A.D1** Evaluate the impact of primary and secondary socialisation on the health and wellbeing of individuals, with reference to relevant examples.
2A.P2 Describe the effects of socialisation on the health and wellbeing of individuals.		
Learning Aim B: Understand the influences that relationships have on the health and wellbeing of individuals		
2B.P3 Describe the influences that different types of relationships have on the health and wellbeing of individuals.	**2B.M2** Explain the influences that different types of relationships have on the health and wellbeing of individuals.	**2B.D2** Compare the potential positive and negative influences of different relationships on the health and wellbeing of individuals.
Learning Aim C: Investigate the effects of social factors on the health and wellbeing of individuals		
2C.P4 Describe how social factors can affect the health and wellbeing of individuals.	**2C.M3** Explain how social factors can affect the health and wellbeing of individuals, with reference to relevant examples.	**2C.D3** Evaluate the link between social factors and the health and wellbeing of individuals, and the impact on health and wellbeing, with reference to relevant examples.

Answers: Unit 4 knowledge recap

Learning aim A

1. Socialisation describes the way we learn how to interact with others in society.
2. Primary socialisation describes how we learn from our close family and carers.
3. Secondary socialisation takes place later when we learn from friends, teachers and the media how to interact with others.
4. Socialisation affects all our interactions with others, but especially gender roles, attitudes, the development of norms and of language, and it also affects lifestyle choices.

break-up. This is stressful for the child, increases their anxiety and may damage their self-esteem as they feel they are no longer worthy of love. This dysfunctional family relationship has a negative impact on health and on wellbeing.

4. A relationship where both people care for each other is an example of a *positive* influence on health and wellbeing.
5. This type of relationship will be destructive for the employee's self-esteem and harmful to health and wellbeing.

Learning aim B

1. Family (for example, extended, nuclear, reconstituted, single-parent); working (for example, teacher/student, colleagues, line managers); social (for example, friends, fellow members of religious and secular groups); and intimate and sexual relationships.
2. A reconstituted family may include children from different marriages, their parent and their step parent when mum or dad remarry or have a new partner.
3. When family relationships break down, the family unit becomes unstable and a child feels insecure and uncertain of their place. They may feel unloved and may blame themselves for the

Learning aim C

1. Twelve social factors t hat influence health and wellbeing are income, education, occupation, social class, wealth, values and behaviours, family, peers, media, living conditions, gender, culture.
2. Social factors may limit what choices people have, or they may widen the choices they have about diet, smoking, living accommodation, use of recreational drugs, alcohol consumption, participation in sport or exercise and seeking medical care.
3. Social factors affect self-esteem, levels of stress and anxiety, access to health and social care services and also physical health.

Index

Index